TO : ....

FROM : ....

TODAY'S DATE : ....

10 9 8 7 6 5 4 3 2 1

Editorial by Sam Hutchinson
Design and illustration by Vicky Barker

ISBN: 978-1-63158-716-0

Printed in China

My MOMMY and ME

A KEEPSAKE ACTIVITY BOOK

WRITTEN BY
SAM HUTCHINSON

ILLUSTRATED BY
VICKY BARKER

FOR
YOUNG
READERS

This is my mommy!

STICK PHOTO
IN HERE!

Her first name is ....

She is .... years old.

This is me!

STICK PHOTO
IN HERE!

My first name is ....

I am .... years old.

My mommy's full name is

....

Her date of birth is

....

She was born in

....

She has .... siblings

Was your mommy born where you live now?
Look up her place of birth on a map
... even if it is only a few streets away!

My full name is

....

My date of birth is

....

I was born in

....

I have .... siblings

Do you know where your name comes from?
Who chose it? Does it have a special meaning?
Design a badge all about your name.

My mommy's height is

....

Her hair color is

....

Her hair length is

....

Her eye color is

....

Draw a picture of your mommy!

My height is

....

My mommy is .... taller than me

My hair color is   My hair length is

....

My eye color is

....

Do you look similar to your mommy?
Do you have the same hair color?
How about your mommy's mommy
(your grandparent!). Do they look similar?

Draw a picture of yourself!
Make sure to sign your drawing,
like a famous artist.

The school my mommy went to is called

....

It is in

....

Her favorite
lesson was

Her least favorite
lesson was

....

....

Did your mommy do any
activities at school
or after school?
Write about them here.

....

....

....

....

Ask your mommy if she
has any photos or
certificates you can see.

My school is called

....

It is in

....

My favorite
lesson is

....

My least favorite
lesson is

....

Do you do any activities at school or after school?
Are they similar to the activities your mommy did?
Write about a time that your mommy helped you
with something at school or after school.

....

....

....

....

During the school day, when I am at school or learning at home, my mommy does

....

....

....

Stick a photo or draw a picture here

Stick a photo or draw a picture here

When mommy was my age she dreamed of being a

....

....

....

When I am my mommy's age I want to be doing ...

My mommy's favorite color is

....

My mommy's favorite
piece of clothing is

....

Design a T-shirt
that you think
your mommy
will love!

My favorite color is

....

My favorite piece
of clothing is

....

Design a piece of clothing that
shows you and you mommy together!

Tell a funny story or draw a comic strip that will make your mommy laugh!

My mommy's favorite song is

....

The name of the band or the singer is

....

The song first came out in

....

My mommy loves this song because

....

....

....

My favorite song is

....

The name of the band or the singer is

....

The song first came out in

....

I love this song because

....

....

....

For breakfast, my mommy likes to eat

....

For lunch, my mommy likes to eat

....

For dinner, my mommy likes to eat

....

Her favorite food is   Her least favorite food is

....

She can cook .... really well!

Draw a picture here

For breakfast, I like to eat

....

For lunch, I like to eat

....

For dinner, I like to eat

....

My favorite food is

....

My least favorite food is

....

I can cook .... really well!

Draw a picture here

Using three different colors, circle words that describe you in one color, words that describe your mommy in another color and, in a third color, circle words that describe you both.

Kind

Funny

Silly

Serious

Outgoing

Fun

Clean

Confident

Friendly

Private

Quiet

Energetic

Caring

Calm

Thoughtful

My perfect day with my mommy would involve:

In the morning,

....

....

....

At lunchtime,

....

....

....

In the afternoon,

....

....

....

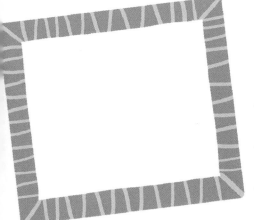

In the evening,

....

....

....

Draw you and your mommy together at the end of a happy day together! You can stick in a photograph if you prefer.

My mommy travels around by

....

Draw a picture of your mommy and her favorite mode of transportation.

When I am my mommy's age,
I will travel around in my

Draw a picture of your futuristic
mode of transport!

My mommy's favorite hobbies include:

....

....

....

....

....

STICK PHOTO
IN HERE!

My favorite hobbies include:

....

....

....

....

....

One thing we love to do together is:

....

One thing we would like to do
together in the future is:

....

Finish writing this poem about your mommy!

I know my mommy loves me
She says it every day ...